AF492563

DIANA WHITE

HOUSE PLANTS: A BEGINNER'S GUIDE to NURTURE and CARE for YOUR INDOOR PLANTS

Copyright © 2022 by diana white

All rights reserved. No part of this publication may be reproduced, stored or transmitted in any form or by any means, electronic, mechanical, photocopying, recording, scanning, or otherwise without written permission from the publisher. It is illegal to copy this book, post it to a website, or distribute it by any other means without permission.

diana white asserts the moral right to be identified as the author of this work.

diana white has no responsibility for the persistence or accuracy of URLs for external or third-party Internet Websites referred to in this publication and does not guarantee that any content on such Websites is, or will remain, accurate or appropriate.

Designations used by companies to distinguish their products are often claimed as trademarks. All brand names and product names used in this book and on its cover are trade names, service marks, trademarks and registered trademarks of their respective owners. The publishers and the book are not associated with any product or vendor mentioned in this book. None of the companies referenced within the book have endorsed the book.

First edition

This book was professionally typeset on Reedsy.
Find out more at reedsy.com

Plants give us oxygen for the lungs and for the soul.

Linda Solegalo

Contents

1

Introduction

Welcome to my guide to nurture and care for your indoor plants. I am very excited to share this information with you. I am a lover of plants as they bring me a great deal of joy and comfort. I love how alive they are and there are so many beautiful plants to choose from. I am fascinated with the different textures of leaves. In Fact just this week as I was out walking and decided to touch a few of the plants I walked past. I noticed that there was a thicker feel to some of them than say some of the plants I have indoors. I live in the United Kingdom and at the moment it is raining cats and dogs. I wondered whether the elements have anything to do with the coarseness of some of the leaves to be able to withstand the elements. I wondered whether they are designed that way to protect them from the harsh weather.

During lockdown I decided to increase my house plants as they can lift your mood and create a soothing atmosphere. People's mental health ranging from students singles, married, family life and the elderly suddenly became highlighted during this time. A number of friends I know also told me how their gardens really helped them through this period as they spent considerable time weeding pruning repotting plants.

I like taking care of my indoor plants by watering them, telling them good morning, gently ruffle them, pruning them, watching them grow and simply admiring them.

My home is in walking distance to a plant shop so it was easier for me to pop in to buy a plant when I initially moved to the area. One plant became two and two became three and before you know it I had a good handful of plants to call my own. Some of them lived a long time and some of them wilted away no matter how I tried to revive them. It's amazing how you can become attached to a plant!

Then over time I realise though that some of these plants take more water than some, some plants require very little attention and this can be good news if I am going a way for a weekend! Also in the same breath if I go away for too long without making arrangements to look after my plants this on the other hand can be problematic for my plants and they wither away. Also, some plants need to be removed from a window sill if it is too windy. Some plants need to be moved to a cooler room to prevent wilting. Again in the winter months if a room is too warm from the heating this can affect plants. My purpose is to share with you how to nurture and care for your indoor plants so that they thrive in most environments!

A little bit more about me is that in line with my love of nature I am also a member of a walking group and we walk mostly on weekends. We walk in local parks and sometimes travel a bit further. I never fail to be fascinated by the different trees, their shapes, the fruits they bear and the rich energy they give off. By the end of the walk I am left feeling energised and ready to take on the world.

I recently got the opportunity to travel on a short trip to an island in the Caribbean and got to experience the island's rich and lush landscape in the warmth of the sun. I was able to see beautiful and rare plants, trees from which hung mouth watering fruits, orchids, different types of palms and it was amazing to see. I could not keep my eyes off of the rich landscape and countryside as I travelled from one town to the next! I also realised that my health improved during the trip and feel that the green environment certainly played apart in this.

My choosing to have indoor plants is my way of bringing nature into my home, my space and my environment. It means I can have them near me no matter the weather outside. Living in the United Kingdom as you may be aware I can experience at times all four seasons in a day - or maybe three. My ability to enjoy my love of nature and the outdoors

- could be greatly affected if I am not able to go outdoors because of the weather. I am really grateful that I can create my space with the soothing effect of indoor plants.

What does your space mean for you? Is it your little bit of heaven here on earth as it is for me? Whether your space is large and expansive or small and compact you can use plants to enhance your environment and create your piece of heaven here on earth.

Indoor plants are not necessarily in their natural environment and so it is important that they are nurtured and cared for in some of the ways I have already mentioned to get the best from them.

My intention is to share with you the reasons why house plants are beneficial to you and why having them in your home can make all the difference in the world.

I will also share some of the best plants to have in your home and generally how to care for them so that they glow and enhance your space. How does that sound? Are you as excited as I am to share this information with you?

If you already have some of the plants mentioned in this book in your home then hopefully using these tips will give you easy access to taking better care of your plants so that they thrive just as if they were out in nature.

2

What are House Plants and Why House Plants?

Welcome to my guide to nurture and care for your indoor plants. I am very excited to share this information with you. I am a lover of plants as they bring me a great deal of joy and comfort. I love how alive they are and there are so many beautiful plants to choose from. I am fascinated with the different textures of leaves.

In Fact just this week as I was out walking and decided to touch a few of the plants I walked past. I noticed that there was a thicker feel to some of them than say some of the plants I have indoors.

I live in the United Kingdom and at the moment it is raining cats and dogs. I wondered whether the elements have anything to do with the coarseness of some of the leaves to be able to withstand the elements. I wondered whether they are designed that way to protect them from the harsh weather.

During lockdown I decided to increase my house plants as they can lift your mood and create a soothing atmosphere. People's mental health ranging from students singles, married, family life and the elderly suddenly became highlighted during this time. A number of friends I know also told me how their gardens really helped them through this period as they spent considerable time weeding, pruning and repotting plants.

I like taking care of my indoor plants by watering them, telling them good morning, gently ruffle them, pruning them, watching them grow and simply admiring them.

My home is in walking distance to a plant shop so it was easier for me to pop in to buy a plant when I initially moved to the area. One plant became two and two became three and before you know it I had a good handful of plants to call my own. Some of them lived a long time and some of them wilted away no matter how I tried to revive them. It's amazing how you can become attached to a plant!

Then over time I realise though that some of these plants take more water than some, some plants require very little attention and this can be good news if I am going a way for a weekend! Also in the same breath if I go away for too long without making arrangements to look after my plants this on the other hand can be problematic for my plants and they wither away. Also, some plants need to be removed from a window sill if it is too windy. Some plants need to be moved to a cooler room to prevent wilting. Again in the winter months if a room is too warm from the heating this can affect plants. My purpose is to share with you how to nurture and care for your indoor plants so that they thrive in most environments!

A little bit more about me is that in line with my love of nature I am also a member of a walking group and we walk mostly on weekends. We walk in local parks and sometimes travel a bit further. I never fail to be fascinated by the different trees, their shapes, the fruits they bear and the rich energy they give off. By the end of the walk I am left feeling energised and ready to take on the world.

I recently got the opportunity to travel on a short trip to an island in the Caribbean and got to experience the island's rich and lush landscape in the warmth of the sun. I was able to see beautiful and rare plants, trees from which hung mouth watering fruits, orchids, different types of palms and it was amazing to see. I could not keep my eyes off of the rich landscape and countryside as I travelled from one town to the next! I also realised that my health improved during the trip and feel that the green environment certainly played apart in this.

My choosing to have indoor plants is my way of bringing nature into my home, my space and my environment. It means I can have them near me no matter the weather outside. Living in the United Kingdom as you may be aware I can experience at times all four seasons in a day - or maybe three. My ability to enjoy my love of nature and the outdoors - could be greatly affected if I am not able to go outdoors because of the weather. I am really grateful that I can create my space with the soothing effect of indoor plants.

What does your space mean for you? Is it your little bit of heaven here on earth as it is for me? Whether your space is large and expansive or small and compact you can use plants to enhance your environment and create your piece of heaven here on earth.

Indoor plants are not necessarily in their natural environment and so it is important that they are nurtured and cared for in some of the ways I have already mentioned to get the best from them.

My intention is to share with you the reasons why house plants are beneficial to you and why having them in your home can make all the difference in the world.

I will also share some of the best plants to have in your home and generally how to care for them so that they glow and enhance your space. How does that sound? Are you as excited as I am to share this information with you?

If you already have some of the plants mentioned in this book in your home then hopefully using these tips will give you easy access to taking better care of your plants so that they thrive just as if they were out in nature.

3

Peace Lilly

The peace lily is such a beautiful and elegant plant and so easy to maintain and enhances the environment. I found out that it got its name from the white flower that looks like flags of peace. What is also more interesting to know is that the plant is a tropical perennial and from a family of almost 50 species - it's actually not a lily. This seems to make sense as they do not look like water lilies!

The peace lily is also easy to care for as an indoor plant and sensitive to cold temperatures. They can grow up to 4 feet in a home.

I have a peace lily in my home and I have had it for the longest while. Whilst it is nowhere near 4 ft it continues to shoot out more leaves from the soil at the base of the stems. I really love to see the new growth as they are crispy brand new, healthy and almost perfectly formed. I have noticed one or two of the leaves on the plant become brown at the edges. I believe this is due to the warm atmosphere from the heating. Have moved it a few times as it may have got too much direct heat in the summer. I tend to pour a little water around the stems of the plant and soil every other day. It is also important to avoid over watering your Peace Lily.

Peace lilies need to be placed in a sunny area and not directly in the sunlight, for example near a window and not in the window where there is direct sun. The soil is to be kept moist. I also use plant food once every two months. I find from experience that giving plants too much plant food can destroy them so be wise in using plant foods.

I have had to repot my peace lily in the past due to overgrowth, so observe how it is growing and repot as necessary. Plant shops usually have deals where you can purchase up to 5 medium size pots at a time with the base plates and these can come in handy for repotting.

Peace lilies are also good for cleaning and purifying the air and are good for bedrooms and living rooms. In saying that a peace lily will grow anywhere you place it.

Another important point to note is that the plant should be kept out of the reach of children as it is a poisonous plant and can cause vomiting/swelling of the tongue if eaten.

Plants tend to grow better when you use pots that are nearer to the size of the root mass of a plant rather than an oversized pot as they will grow better.

Be aware of insects and fungus that can invade a plant.

To manage dust use a damp cloth to wipe down as thick layers of dust can affect photosynthesis. Wiping plants will also help to prevent insects and fungus that can invade it.

Are there any signs of yellow leaves on your peace lily? This is likely to mean that the plant is being over-watered. Reduce the water used and this may mean you stop applying water for a period of time and watching how the plant is growing.

Brown edges on a plant? Your plant is receiving too many direct rays of the sun. Move the plant to a more shaded area of your home.

No blooms showing? Your plant needs more light, move it to a brighter location to encourage flowering.

4

Indoor Palm

I ndoor palms are equally beautiful tropical plants that can be quite decorative enhancing the ambience of a room or space. There are about 2,600 species of palm trees most of which originate in South America, Asia and the Caribbean. That's quite a lot of palms to choose from right? You will be pleased to know that just under 10 of these plants can grow indoors.

The bigger plants are usually seen at entrances or public places and the smaller ones used in homes. I recall seeing palms on special occasions placed on platforms such as weddings, funerals and other celebrations and functions. They bring a calming, celebratory effect to the atmosphere and this atmosphere can also be transported into your home. So if you like the jungle effect then it can be brought into your home.

Indoor palms are to be kept out of direct sunlight which can cause dryness. They will also thrive in a humid environment.

Some of the best indoor palm plants to grow at home are:

- Palor Palm (Chamaedorea elegans)
- Yucca Palm (Yucca elephantines)
- Magestic Palm (Ravenea rivularis)
- Cascade Palm (Chamaedorea cataractarum)
- Arcca Palm (Dypsis lutescens)
- Chines Fan Palm (Livistona chinensis)
- Ponytail Palm (Beaucarnea recurvata)
-

The Areca Palm (Dypsis lutescens) also known as the bamboo plant is a popular lush elegant plant. It is one of the many indoor plants that thrives best out of direct sunlight to prevent damage to its delicate leaves.

The process of nurturing a new palm is to water it every day for a week and then every other day the next week. Once it settles it can be watered 2-3 times a week.

Brown leaves on a palm could be down to under watering it so this also needs to be monitored.

5

Aloe Vera Plant

Most of us know the aloe vera plant as a succulent plant due to its thick jelly interior which is used in lot of skincare products due to it's health giving properties. It is also used in drinks and smoothies for the same reason.

These plants generally grow best as an indoor plant and can also be placed outside in summer months. There are about 500 species of the Aloe Vera plant and some are more favoured than some. They require bright and indirect light. Due to it being a succulent plant they can be watered once every three weeks. Watch the water intake and if it is quite wet allow it to dry out before watering it again.

Bright sun and infrequent watering will help the plant to thrive.

Good facts to know are that the leaves can be propagated by replanting the leaves/pups and making sure the base of it is covered with soil. It can take a few months before it grows root.

Using a soft cloth to wipe away dust will also help in keeping insects and fungus at bay.

6

Money Plant

The money plant or lucky plant has a number of other names it is known by. Other popular names it is known by are Crassula Ovata and jade plant. These are popular and current plants to add to one's home as they are simple to maintain. I like to keep things simple and prefer the name money plant.

They are called succulent plants native to South Africa and Zimbabwe.

Apparently it used to be a lot more popular in the past than it is today. It seems to have come full circle as it is relatively popular in today's day and age. I have them and really love having them around. I believe it has its origin in Feng Shui and China which in a nutshell means it has a harmonising effect on one's surrounding environment. I have certainly seen them in most Chinese take away shops.

These plants can live for many years and require a lot of natural light to thrive however can still thrive in shady areas of a home.

As a succulent plant they tend to have toughness about them and therefore adaptable to different environments. Water them and allow the soil to dry before watering them again. In winter months use even less water so that the soil is just moist. You can also feed it with general houseplant food.

Be mindful of the cold weather as if it gets too cold it will cause it to die.

7

Snake Plant (Sanserieria)

The snake plant is a popular indoor plant and requires little maintenance. As the name suggests it looks snake-like both in the colouring/texture and because they grow straight up.

Other names are viper's bowstring hemp and St George's sword. It is a strong plant that is not very easy to kill, as you can see the leaves are quite thick.

They can survive in both bright sunlight and dark corners of a room. They do not require much water. It thrives in warm weather and can go without water for up to two months. In warmer weather water every fortnight.

8

Swiss Cheese Plant (Monstera Deliciosa)

The swiss cheese plant is a beautiful plant that can allow your environment and space to pop. It is also known as the split leaf philodendron. Other names for it are window leaf and ceriman. I love the shape and design of the leaves which have holes or splits in them. The leaves can grow quite big and lush. It is native to Central America.

They require very little maintenance and thrive in warm humid weather and prefer bright light. It requires regular watering every one to two weeks and much less in the winter months. The plant is toxic to pets and should be borne in mind.

Yellow leaves indicate the soil is dry. Prune and remove the wilted leaves.

9

Devil's Ivy (Pothos)

T his is a very low maintenance plant of which I have had some experience. I am considering cutting mine which has grown quite long and I decorate it around my t.v. and other objects at home. I love it, though and am in two minds about cutting it. I have two different types growing at home. They can be tangled if left to grow and a useful tip is to shake them out to detangle it. Also if they are left unattended it can attract insects so it is important to keep an eye on it.

The plant likes bright light and can thrive in shady areas as well. It will indicate when it needs to be watered as it is a resilient plant. If the edges are brown this means it was not watered sufficiently. The plant likes high humidity. What I love about this plant is that it is very forgiving if left unwatered for a few days). When watered it comes back to life again.

10

Spider Plant (Chloropylum Cosmosum)

T he spider is a beautiful plant that is robust and can grow through different kinds of conditions. It has some similarity with photos plant in this way.

It likes the sun and will thrive also in shady areas as well. It is one of those plants that you can leave for a long time and come back to as it will still be alive and grow! They are also easy to maintain and therefore make a brilliant house plant.

As the name suggests the plant has beautiful and variegated foliage growing out from the root that look like the legs of a spider.

I remember as a child growing up my brother would uproot similar looking plants and try to scare me with it. I in turn would run crying to my mother as I was terrified of the way the plant looked with the dirt around the root and the spider looking leaves. Back then it represented something completely different! I look at a spider plant today and see so much delicate beauty, especially when they are hanging in a kitchen.

It's a beautiful plant flowering in the spring and summer. They can also grow outside in summer months. It is recommended that you move them back in doors in the autumn months where the weather becomes cooler and frostier.

In caring for the plant ensure that it is watered regularly and at the same time be mindful of overwatering it. The foliage can be misted with water to prevent brown tips of the leaves.

11

Rubber plants (Ficus Elastica)

Do you know the rubber plant? Well it is another plant that you can get away without watering for a while. It makes a really beautiful house plant. Generally though the soil will need to stay moist and the leaves appreciate being sprayed with water. It likes sunlight however keep it from direct sunlight as this will destroy the plant.

Another thing to bear in mind is that the plant likes humid conditions and without it the leaves tend to fall off.

Ever notice yellow leaves on a plant? You will need to ease off watering it as you are giving it too much water. Proper care of your house plants means they get to live up to 10 years! They are definitely worth all the care and nurture they need to thrive.

Another important thing to bear in mind is to have well drained soil. Rotting of roots is a major issue for indoor plants. Roots can rot if water stagnates so it is important that water is allowed to pass through the soil at a moderate pace without pooling and puddling. Soils that drain too quickly means plants do not have sufficient time to absorb the water and can die.

12

Anthurium

Anthuriums with the red heart shaped flower with the red stem protruding from it can be a delight to behold as it adds a dash of colour to a home. It's a cheerful and stable plant to have in one's home.

Anthuriums are definitely one of the plants that seem to thrive through all four seasons. They are also described by a number of names such as the flamingo flower, flamingo lily or laceleaf. I learnt that there are over 1,000 species!

I bought one for my sister a few years ago when she was unwell and she placed it in a very sunny window in her living room and it thrived! It grew to such an extent that I had to re-pot it into a much bigger pot and it continued to produce the beautiful heart shaped flowers. It just kept growing and churning out shoots of leaves and red flowers. Every time I visited (which was quite often at one point), I loved observing the many newly formed tiny red flowers unfold into full grown red flowers. It was great watching the plant flower and really cheered up the room. I eventually repotted it into three different pots and placed them in different places in her apartment. I did notice that once they were moved from the window sill that it did not produce as many flowers as before.

They still thrive in the cooler areas and every now and again I would place them near sunlight and move them back to their previous places after a few days. I also had to watch how much water I gave them as over watering can affect the health of the plant.

Anthurium, also known as the flamingo flower, flamingo lily, boy flower, oilcloth flower or laceleaf, is an exotic-looking indoor plant with a red flower, and large, glossy leaves. Its name is derived from two Greek words, anthos (flower) and oura (tail), hence another of its common names, tail flower.

Anthurium flowers are actually 'spathes' – brightly coloured leaves that attract insects in the wild. The flower is actually the central 'spadix', made up of lots of tiny blooms. The blooms appear intermittently throughout the year and last for between six to eight weeks, with a 'rest period' of up to three months in between.

I understand that there are over 1,000 varieties of the plant available. The most common one is the Anthurium andreanum which has heart shape leaves and shiny leave a popular plant in some caribbean Islands.

13

Orchids

O rchids are another set of plants that make good house plants. Some words used to describe them are charming", "beautiful" "refinement" and "fertility." Apparently they were once reserved for the wealthy and rich. Today they are far more easily accessible.

They come in a wide variety including in colours which can include white, yellow, pink, red orange purple and blue. I also understand that the blue orchid is the rarest! Beware of the fake ones where a blue dye is added to make them look similar to the original blue ones.. Sometimes there is more than one colour on one plant - so beautiful. They also tend to have a lot of blooms on them and when they decide to bloom the sight is amazing to behold. I take pictures of them and send them to family and friends!

Easy orchids to grow are the Lady of the Night, Jewel Orchid, Nun's orchid, Dendrobium and the Pansy orchids.

Buds that are unopened are sensitive to touch and it is important that hands are washed thoroughly before handling the plant.

Care for orchids really does depend on the species however and a general rule of thumb is to water once a week and up to 10 days.

I got a rude awakening from another sister, also a plant lover. I used to water my orchid every few days and at one point was watering it almost every day. She gave me a scolding (she likes to scold). Since following her advice to make sure the saucer/wate holder is dry before watering I see an improvement in my orchids. I also recall that they bloomed for a long period of the summer months and felt a certain disappointment when the delicate white petals began to fall off. Then the two long stems from which the buds had grown became hard wood even though the big floppy leaves at the bottom continued to thrive and began to produce a leaf in the middle of it.

Orchids require indirect sunlight and watering them with ice cubes helps them to bloom! Place them in a cooler place at night.

Plants, the soil, gardening can bring so much joy. They not only bring joy they also bring healing and restoration. I would even go so far as to say that tending to them can give you a new lease on life. I would encourage anyone who is feeling unwell to take up gardening if they are able to.

14

Conclusion

I have an uncle who is 97 years old. A few years ago his doctor sent him home to live out the remainder of his life in the next 6 months due to a heart condition that they could not cure. One thing he loves is his gardening.

He spent a lot of time in his garden during the summer months tending to his plants - flowers, fruit trees and some vegetables. His health improved with a lot of care from his family. He lived another year and another and another and another and he is alive a well today.

I believe that in addition to care from his family, his health improved due to his connection with the earth, the soil, and gardening. His health turned completely around and he is alive and well today. He is truly a miracle. As he found pleasure in nurturing the plants in his garden. He himself was nurtured back in his health.

There is definitely something about the soil and human connection that contributes to renewing our wellbeing as human beings and give us a new lease on life. Why would you not want to nurture and care for your plants?

We can spend time in nature and the outdoors taking in all the goodness that plant life brings to our wellbeing. We can go a step further and bring nature and plants into our homes too. In doing so we must also take care of them to ensure they thrive and grow as they bring us benefits too.

www.ingramcontent.com/pod-product-compliance
Lightning Source LLC
Chambersburg PA
CBHW072131150726

47999CB00005B/2239